Let's Go to Japan!

日本

*To my dear friend Hirai, international salesman
by day, by descent a samurai.* — 好朋友

*Artist: Michael Blendermann
Editor: Geoff Smith
Illustrations: Inscribe Graphics*

Copyright © 2015 by Tommy Tong
ISBN: Hardback – 978-1-940827-13-1
ISBN: Ebook – 978-1-940827-17-9
ISBN: Kindle – 978-1-940827-18-6

During the Stone Age tens of thousands of years ago, people made their way across Asia in search of new lands to feed their families, grow their tribes and live in peace. It was a time when most people in the world still lived in caves or small huts and used rocks for tools.

Asia

The seas were not as high back then, so people were able to walk to the lands that are now called Japan.

Pacific Ocean

Eventually the ocean levels rose, and Japan became a chain of islands. (There are 6,852 islands to be exact, but most of them are too small for people to live on.)

The Japanese enjoyed their rich land, eating walnuts, salmon, oysters, seaweed, and many other foods that nature provided.

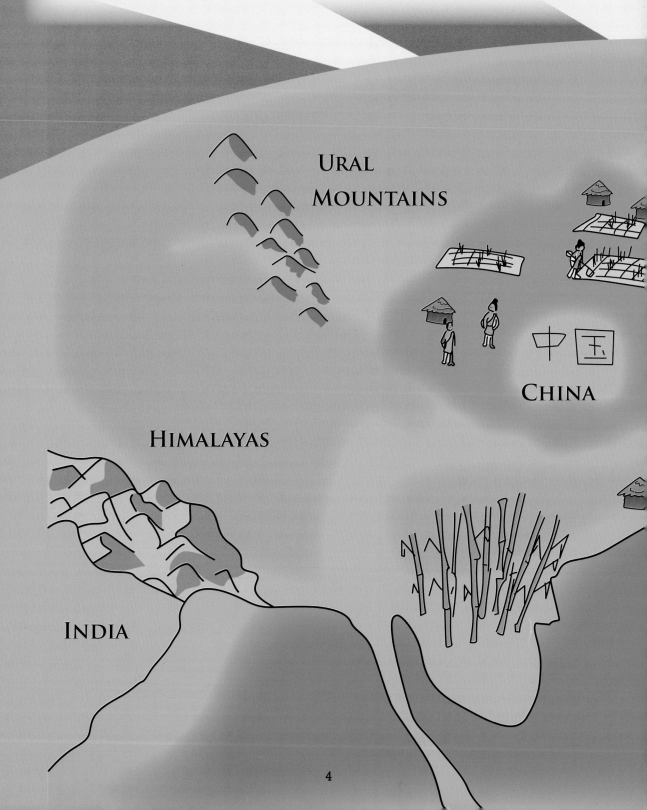

URAL
MOUNTAINS

CHINA

HIMALAYAS

INDIA

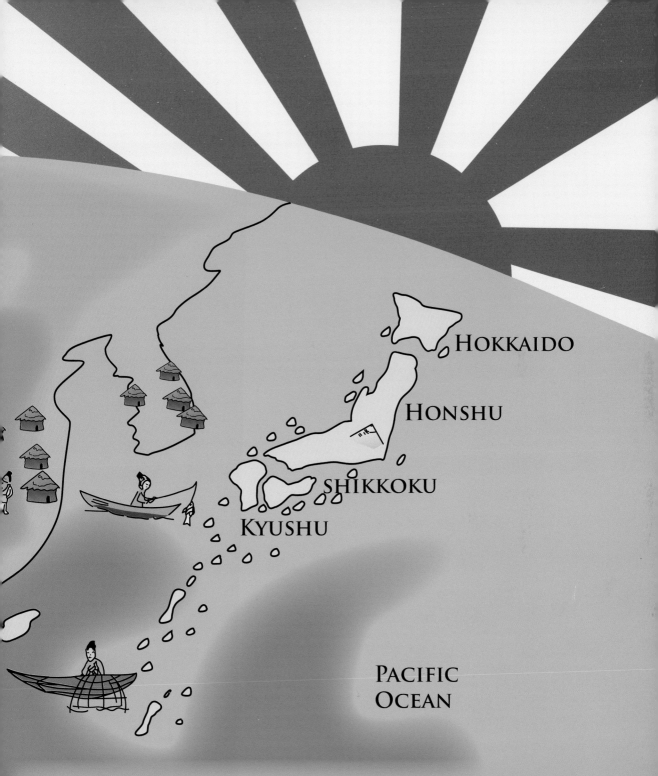

HOKKAIDO

HONSHU

SHIKKOKU

KYUSHU

PACIFIC
OCEAN

The Japanese thought their home was where the sun first came up every morning so they named the islands "Land of the Rising Sun." Can you name the four biggest islands of Japan?

The rest of the world soon forgot about the islands, because they were hundreds of miles from the mainland. Sails for rafts and boats had not been invented yet, so if you drifted out too far from the mainland it was not possible to row back home against the strong ocean currents.

SHIKK

KYUSHU

While little is known about Japan's early history, we do know that they had pottery over ten thousand years ago.

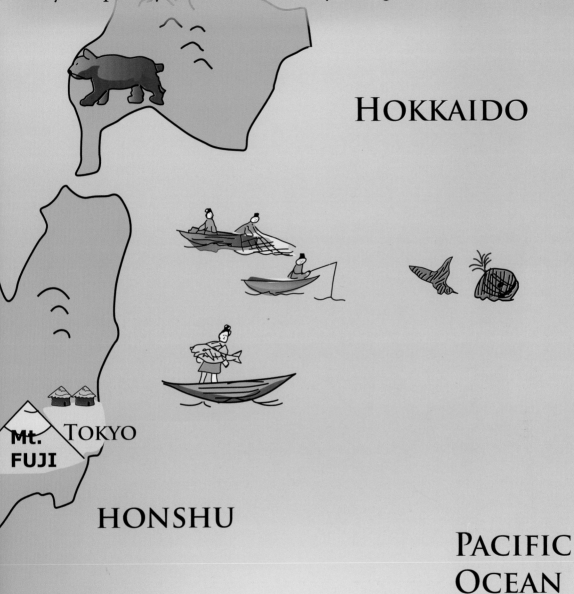

HOKKAIDO

Mt.
FUJI TOKYO

HONSHU

PACIFIC
OCEAN

Pottery allowed people to cook more foods, but the people of Japan still liked to eat many things raw. They hunted pigs, fished for tuna and dove for all kinds of shellfish.

Japan's first emperor was a powerful and wise man named Jimmu. He lived more than 2,500 years ago and led his armies across the islands of Japan to unite the people into one country for the first time.

The Japanese still honor Emperor Jimmu every year on the country's birthday.

Japan has had many emperors since then and still has one today. But today's emperor is not as powerful as the emperors before him and like many other modern kings, he is no longer in charge of the country.

Surrounded by ocean and far from shore, Japan was safe from invaders for many years to come. Their cities grew and the people prospered. They created rules for people to follow and became very polite to one another.

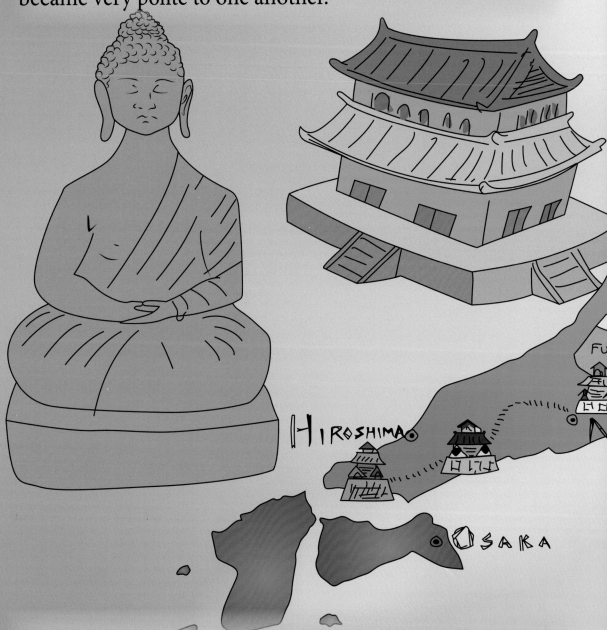

Soon they had great palaces, fine arts and temples across the land to honor the gods for creating their wonderful islands.

Japanese temples are called *Shinto Shrines* and are places where gods and spirits can stay when they visit Earth. Have you ever seen one of these temples before?

For thousands of years the Japanese followed their Shinto faith and honored the spirits of nature in their own special way. When the teachings of Buddha came to the islands in 500 A.D., the Japanese put the two religions together and kept them both.

Today there are Shinto shrines and Buddhist temples all over Japan. Most Japanese believe both ways of thinking, making their Buddhist practices different from any other country in the world.

In order to keep Japan safe from foreign invaders and maintain peace across the land, emperors kept small armies of samurai. These highly trained soldiers had the finest swords in the world and were very dedicated to the "ways of the warrior."

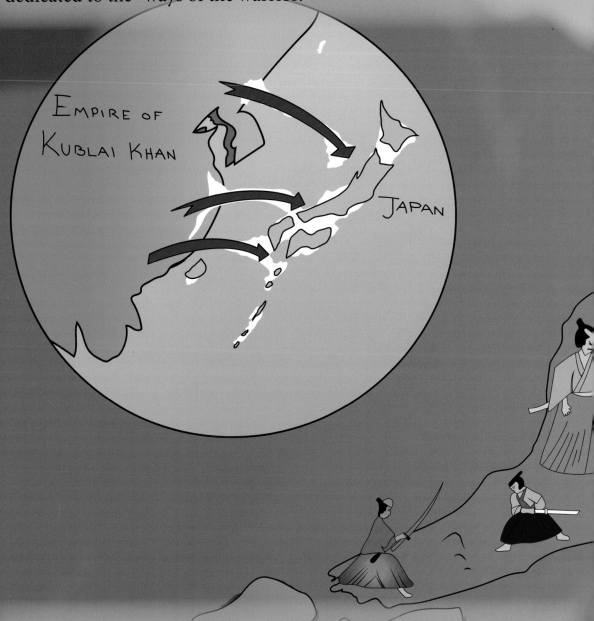

Samurai means "servant," and their code of honor is called "Bushido." They became the most respected class of people in Japan because of their hard work and intense loyalty to their masters.

The emperor called his top samurai master a "shogun" - that means "first military commander" in Japanese.

With the help of Japan's violent storms and huge ocean waves called "tsunamis", the shoguns defeated all invading armies including the Mongolian empire that swept over everything else in its path.

The Shoguns became the most powerful men in Japan and even began to control the emperors. Sometimes the masters of different clans would fight each other in order to become the Shogun.

Other times they would capture the emperor and force him to make them the shogun, but they never made themselves emperors.

The last great war between samurai clans ended more than 400 years ago when a man named Tokugawa united Japan once and for all. The Tokugawa clan ruled Japan up until modern times.

When a samurai lost his master, sometimes he would wander the land from town to town looking for work, protecting the weak and trying to create a new life.

These samurai were called "Ronin" and were not treated well or respected. They were sworn to be loyal to their masters, and people thought that if their master had died in battle, the samurai should have died as well.

宮本武蔵

One of the most famous Ronin was a man named Musashi. He became known as the best swordsman to ever live. People from all over the land came to meet him, study from him, and even fight him so they could become famous too.

Musashi beat everyone who ever fought him and became so good that he even stopped using a sword so he would not hurt his foolish attackers. He would use broom handles, boat oars, and even tree branches to beat them even though they all used their swords!

Musashi was very famous, but he wanted to be left alone and not have to fight people all the time. He moved from town to town trying to hide from those who might know him.

He finally found a cave in the mountains where he could hide and retired to write his thoughts in *The Book of Five Rings*. The book soon became very famous as well and is still read by generals all over the world today.

The shoguns kept the doors of Japan closed. They didn't allow their people to make big ships and burned the ships of new people who arrived. They liked their culture just as it was.

Meanwhile, the rest of the world shared ideas, learned how to make much better ships, and put very powerful guns on them. The Japanese called ships from the west "Black Ships" because of the dark pitch on their hulls that protected the wood for long journeys.

One day a young new country from the other side of the Pacific Ocean sent its powerful warships to Japan. The fleet was commanded by Matthew Perry of the United States of America.

Perry's mission was to force open Japan's doors and rescue stranded sailors who had not been allowed to return to their own countries. Admiral Perry caused a very big and sudden change in Japan's history.

The Japanese saw the incredible power of the Western countries and were struck with fear. Emperor Meiji decided to make peace with the United States and learn everything he could from the West. The mighty shogun was forced to retire and new generals took his place to lead a new kind of army.

The new army used guns instead of swords, bought cannons from the West, and learned new ways of fighting. Soon the samurai began to fade away and those who resisted were swept away by the powerful modern army.

There are only a few samurai left in Japan today. They still secretly practice with their swords and continue to follow their code of honor. Maybe you have met a samurai and didn't even know it!

Japan is about the size of the West Coast of the United States. It also happens to be the same latitude with similar seasons and weather. That means that is has lots of snow in the mountains in winter and plenty of sun on the beaches in summer.

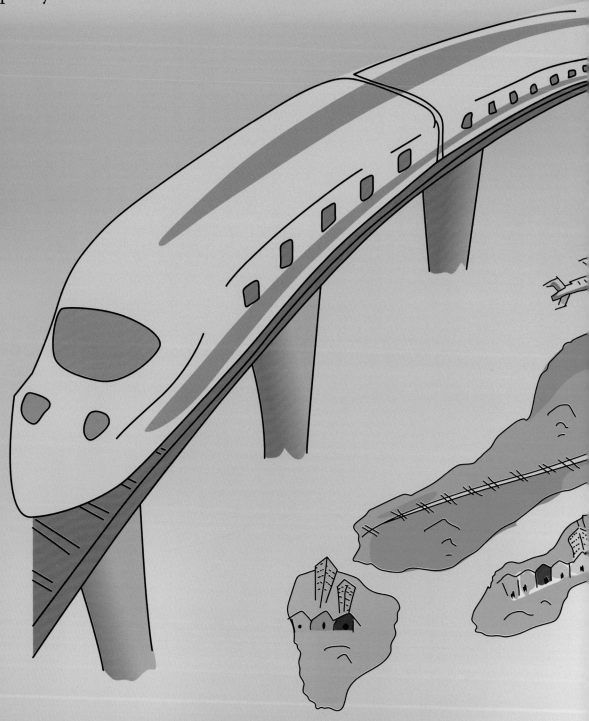

Even though Japan is not a big country, its people work very hard and have made it one of the richest and most advanced nations in the world. Many other countries in Asia try to be like Japan so that they too can be just as rich and famous someday.

Japan doesn't have as many people as its huge neighbor China, but it still has the tenth-largest population in the world. And because Japan is not very big, that makes it even more crowded than China!

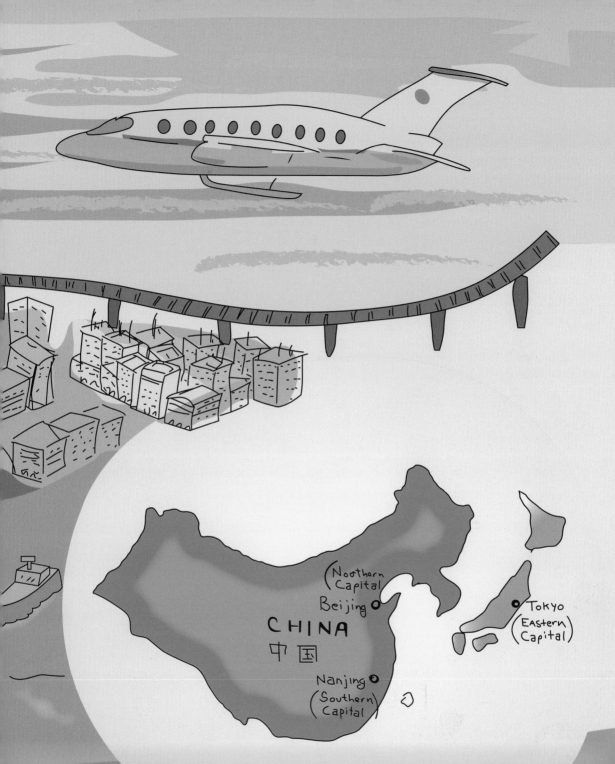

Tokyo is Japan's capital and is the largest city in the world with more than 35 million people living in and around it. Tokyo means "Eastern Capital." Do you know where the Northern and Southern Capitals of Asia are?

Although the Japanese have huge cities, build bullet trains that can go hundreds of miles per hour, and make some of the best cars and electronics in the world, they have not forgotten their traditions.

Many Japanese people still pray at shrines and feel a deep connection to nature. If you go to Japan, don't just visit Tokyo—explore their beautiful mountains, forests, and coasts too!

About the Author

After military service, Tommy did some of his graduate work in Tokyo to study the most powerful international economic forces on the planet at the time. Japan was on fire and expected to soon surpass the US in GNP. Returning to Japan as a businessman, Tommy's military, academic and economic doubts of such an occurrence were soon reinforced by the social and logistical lessons he was to learn there.

Overtaking the US economic superpower was simply not feasible by the small island-nation, yet many westerners continued to preach of the looming period when 'Japan ruled the world'. With its low crime rates, clean streets, familial bonds and over-the-top etiquette, the failed prophecy is forgivable. It truly is an amazing country!

Tommy has learned that over time societies adopt a national psyche and spirit that best fits who they really are as a people. There are still many countries working through the fundamental and often violent stages of self-definition, and ocean currents will forever erode our footings. That said, the Japanese have been deliberately isolating and refining themselves longer than any other major civilization in existence today. Perhaps it warrants a gander, no?

Look for other amazing titles by Tommy Tong...

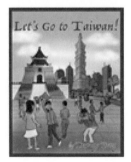